Building Alexandria

Poems

Clarissa Adkins

LILY POETRY REVIEW BOOKS

Copyright © 2021 by Clarissa Adkins

Published by Lily Poetry Review Books
223 Winter Street
Whitman, MA 02382

https://lilypoetryreview.blog/

ISBN: 978-1-7365990-2-0

All rights reserved. Published in the United States by Lily Poetry Review Books.
Library of Congress Control Number: 2021934444

Cover Art: *Bird with a Briefcase* by Matt Lively (mattlively.com)

Design: Martha McCollough

You would like it now, this snow, this hour.
                Your visitation here tonight not altogether unexpected.

                          from "Freedom of Speech" by Lucie Brock-Broido

Contents

1	**Components for a Perfect Life I**
2	Experiment of a Woman as a Paper Cut-out
3	219 Address Street
4	Fishing-kids' Rock Seat
5	Mustard Originelle
7	Building Alexandria
9	Other Than the Middle Child
13	**Components for a Perfect Life II**
14	Date Night
15	Happy Birthday Myself
16	Halloween Lychee
17	Not Just for Eve
18	On Being Phased Out
19	Woman Loses Her Lover
20	A Reopening
21	Living Out of Jars
22	They Don't Want to Get This
27	**Components for a Perfect Life III**
28	Rhubarbs Between Roses
29	Prayer
30	Dying Country
31	Productive
32	Progression
33	Before She Got Away
35	Good Girl
39	**Components for a Perfect Life IV**
40	Recognized as Insect Elsewhere
41	American Concubine
42	For Modernism: First Impressions of War
43	Spores on Postcards
45	To Avoid Vacuuming

49	**Components for a Perfect Life V**
50	Welling Up
51	Elongation
53	Elegy for the Bird Killed in the Parking Lot at St. Edward the Confessor's
54	During the Variety Show
55	Passing by the Lichgate
56	Tracking the Storm
57	From the Third-floor Apartment
59	Pretending to Be a Stingray
60	Lava Song
62	Notes
63	Acknowledgements

For Katherine, Daniel, and Eric

In memory of Lenora Lupo

Building Alexandria

Components for a Perfect Life, Part I

Because of the hours we spend
outside of otherworldly evenings,
sleeping by TVs that never
solve the mysteries of the pyramids

we should make a list of our most
mutable moments, request
from Fortuna, herself, her repetition
of Palladian sunsets

or at least what money does not buy,
so once a week we'd be freed,
inebriated goddesses, enthroned
by campfires and silver wolves

satisfied and sleeping in leaf light,
magnolia, wood, and sap, tempering
our air with Orphic weather for dancing.
We'd wear togas of luminous balzarine.

Experiment of a Woman as a Paper Cut-out

Where they dissect you,
Where the incision begins
    in the story of you,
When in retrospect,
    your eyes inspected the hatches
    across your scalpeled skin,
    part a thing, a sketch, a someone else
    musing about yourself
When you propped near a purple myrtle's
    disjointed limb
    considering petals, not fair,
When after committed
    with workable fixative,
    you stood on the sidewalk—
    your ideas of balloons
    and animals drawn into life,
    held there as you are, in your story
    almost unbelievable, just large as life,
    a fair, fairly believable maiden.

219 Address Street

Survival used to look like any reasonable location.
Now she leans over her foundation's dead spot.
Now survival comes in reaper
black, and rotten dollar, in conundrum
coin and violence.

Survival in hush-blue trim in a brushed
nickel faucet, double sinks, survival
in 1.5 baths and a sunroom
with hundreds of designers to remodel her.

If they knew how much she looked
at leaving, they'd take her away themselves.

If she let her hair hang in her eyes just so, like icy
locks dangling from the frame of a New England
storm window, or like matted too-South kudzu,
she might shut any open door accidentally.

May she escape without letting him squeeze
the going from her throat.
Somebody make her, please, not want
to be any other woman.

Fishing-kids' Rock Seat

    To throw the dead fish heads to
to fight like bog children
              trident for the throne the molded ash and soil
    an insect's grand estate as a little
                          fisherman's seat
it could still be there and the path to the lake

did taller trees like the patch to the right of the marsh find root
          near the pyramid seat

      the concrete mountain   awkward
        it was uneasy to make

the hop   just over the tide of water   for the rock pile builders
            built it   a concocted tower   like a wasp mound
      regal for marching fish-catch kids   the boldest child

would have weaved through brush   if it were now   then

to avoid the flooded muds by the wood   swampiest by the water where

      kids also caught snapping turtles

could have been with a shoe and a hook   but no bacon   no worms
         no Star Crunch Little Debbie's for kid fishers   the patch of lake ignored

        no kids would go in
      but now think   it's all those woods now   all over

grown   so the path is a different shape

      and the swamp has roots.

Mustard Originelle

Pungents of acidic honey appear
like lava—glowing shadows along wood panel—
I sit in an amalgam of bucket wenge armchairs

and think no toes ever fully scoured
the ochre of shag carpet
or the paprika of 1973 family rooms

the teak in its circles
and modern lines—Artiforts and Vissers—
mid-century glossed into retro

disguised as body knowledge—
human cubism—
I can almost dip my hands in the canary

and coat the tandem chairs—
warp Sears catalogues into dandelion
wallpaper, into tri-levels and split-levels

burnt yellow kitchen countertops
astringent painted upon us
the children—

stuck to these fiberglass chairs
our knit-tweed pants sharing wool
with this latter-day Dijon

—we were often left alone—
smeared with Harvest Gold
stirred by cadmium's evolution

sprouting in our jars—which once contained
hexavalent chromium—an orange-tinged
whisky color named National School Bus—spooned

thick onto buses—debuted 1939
the first sulfur spark of pencil-yellow No. 2s—
septic decades irritating each vinegar seam.

Building Alexandria

Artisans still raise the curbs of D.C.
after more than 200 years
into new Alexandrias. In 1978, her mother
held her little, old hand as they walked

to buy groceries across the street, then returned
to the Brutalist apartment—slab-brown brick; metal
tube railings; erratic edges of flat-mud beige—and just beyond
the neighborhood compound, contractors groomed sites

prepped them into mounds of orange,
iron-rich clay—future shopping center plots,
to one day soon, shoot up from the bog,
a sarcophagus city ascending from excavators.

The mother let her climb one of the dirt hills,
where maybe she saw the phallus of Washington
in the distance. Before the child could reach the top,
several boys, kinging the cap, kicked down the just-dry soil

until it avalanched into her mouth,
her eyes. She didn't know where
her mother was as she panicked—
not knowing was just a part of the 70s.

She climbed with other kids, after mass, on corrosion
barrier ramps, at the lower exit of Queen of the Apostles—
a Vatican II, stained-glass colossus. But soon,
parents would yell it wasn't built to be a playground.

On the way home they'd stop at the white-washed
Evan's department store and the little thrift shop
hid along the tiny strip raised in the 50s.
And this store, nameless in her memory

hypnotized her with its selector motion display case—
press forward, press back,
a level of jewelry, a level of coins,
a layer of watches, buttons of Vote for Nixon, Vote for Ike.

They wouldn't ever buy anything,
but she always kept pushing the buttons,
that motion forward, that motion back,
the tie clips and oxidized lockets—one folding

one upon the other, disappearing—dizzying
like the citron and magenta,
paisley dress on the headless mannequin
at the back of the store, a sentry remnant of the 60s.

Maybe the masons once passed the antique coins
from hand to hand, buying and bullying
fresh Alexandria into existence—
That terra must have turned

more than a hundred times her footing up the hill
and still rotates and recycles to the top today,
one building comes down for another—
but never recedes enough for the child to breathe.

Other Than the Middle Child

The barnacle is ever water-logged

at its sea-cramped center—

ever designated as sea-tick,

but is always more abalone, less bloody—

secretes perfect empathy

for lobsters, not asking,

just nodding and winking,

how it does,

to crabs and gulls, taking slap

after slap from the kelp snaps

and seaweed folds.

Still this appendage

never asks permission

to hang on to the metal

of boat or the slate of rock.

It wants but does not say it wants.

Like the underside of attachment,

forever a shadowy flunky, free

to fracture—or detach—

to be the stony suckle of sucklessness.

And the ocean, as family, will heal its back.

Components for a Perfect Life, Part II

Because we believe we don't ask for a lot:
just for our most beloved animals
to tell us in words when they are dying.
To have hair for a spell of eleven weeks

as golden as a summer ghost.
For love to be more than blood
and ion chemistry. To quarter Virginia
into sixty years of four seasons

without its fickle rounds.
Because we rather humility
be the weather of bonfires
that collapse their embers

into slow-motion Jenga. We'd never
be lush when leaving the party. We'd never
have the muse scream we've made waste of her
and say so in the lilt of our voices.

Date Night

I wouldn't call the image a true desire.
It was a flash
of red and rage.

No, *of course* I don't
want to see the pilsner
break like a shower
of Waterford over your head.

But when you mocked my crying
after having made me cry,
I saw myself stand up to you

like a woman
with a weapon.

After that vision,
of course my hands were empty.

Happy Birthday Myself

My birthday still sits by the chrome legs
of orange-flower, vinyl chairs
and the candles: four,
play above, their light upon the cake.

I'm learning about tradition.
I am wide open.

I was wide open.
The world invited me
and then it rescinded.

Once, I belonged outside
on the pink-patterned blanket
in the photograph
and felt how air wove itself
like sutures through the locks
of my baby-head beacon.
I saw that all was happy.

I wish to give those candles back,
                          snuffed.

Halloween Lychee

Your mother still wishes she'd tried your idea
for Halloween punch when you were ten.

Do you remember? Float the lychees
like eyeballs in grape juice.

You pictured them
molding both inside and outside

like milky periscopes,
the peel decaying into salt.

When you're ready to eat the lychee,
carefully strip off its skin.

Imagine the Komodo dragon
stretching its scales between its claws

then cut into the slick, sweet-rotten and eat,
you may find the lizard mineral.

Thank you for having dinner with your mother,
who will throw away the lychee pits and husks for you.

Think of her later, when you're a young man,
rising from the bitter spirits.

Not Just for Eve

True cleanliness is actually only something one feels
                                    when biting an apple.

Being pure requires an empty palette and recall
                                    of feeding on this fruit.

But all these apples make slightly different dins
                                    as if no one's ever learning,

and since no one seems to wash the body as well as one washes the apple's
                                    I forget how simple it is to believe

in one's godliness—how virtue's apportioned by hearing the shovel
                                    shearing top layers of snow

into level ice below—or by letting my cold fingers manipulate pine buds
                                    into early needles.

To witness these sounds is to audit nature for fruit's features, to wash the entire body
                                    once and for all—to be the experience of apple's

pitch—then be red and serene in the snow after it has fallen—when trodden steps
                                    cut time away

into the clout of dead wood—a heavenly quiet caught
                                    between rubber boot and cloud.

One must desire the honey juice to radiate pureness into bursting upon the biting.
                                    Tranquility can always be done this well.

On Being Phased Out

I think you could use a walk separate from me,
along the concrete path, to consider the changes

>that come for the one who is sick
>and the ones who must tend to them.

>It's better you think about this alone.

Because if we walk together
and stop to watch a mother gardening,

>>we might hear her particular song
>>and watch the way she weeds,

how she's creating another space where she is necessary.

I would want so much to hum softly, too,
the song this other mother hums: I won't be phased out yet.

It will bother us, the mother's tilling,
her child on the path strapped in her stroller,
the transient, needy cheeks,
while the mother mulches for flowers.

>>>We won't want to hear the cry of the child
>>>over losing days with her mother,

while her mother is still so healthy and crucial   and her song so solid

>and all of us knowing, we are minute to minute dying.

You wouldn't want to know the words I sing—the secondary fears
that come with every illness—

>you wouldn't want to know into what I've buried the bulbs.

Woman Loses Her Lover

      A black and yellow framed Zenith,
           centered on her
           chest, broadcasts
           the small city at night:

She stays awake, watching.
Plastic signs draw her eyes up
      to the top of the screen,
      five, six, seven stories,
      at every level, characters in neon—
      Kanji, English, and Katakana,
      studios for dance, offices
      for graphic design, for taxes,
      for real estate.
The camera pans to shadowy living—
      her loneliness, anyone's or his,
           hands ringing under Pachinko lighting;
        absence highlighted by vended, packaged dinners;
cigars and sake; the odors wafted and forgotten—
      on the cherry-sour breezes.

      She switches the channel,
of the Zenith:
           watches the story you told her
           about your friend—a static ending.

She suffocates under that TV, cold, too,
      exposed to the judgment, dead weight

      and all who they think

      and all who think they,

           for love's sake, turn to wretchedness.

A Reopening

The farmhouse table is abiding oblivious
in the overgrown forest.

The oak legs dig into dirt
with the girth of Easter dinner.

Roots lace and goose between the stripes
and linens.

Porcelain platters of carrot cake
indulge the floweret dust.

Bugs petrify in tunnels nibbled into pastel eggs:
caves of long-lost covenants.

The guests are sitting statuesque,
while inside they've succumbed to disease.

Their hope dwelled in the ham, congealed now,
while folded hands wove fingers into rotting steeples.

At the ever-Easter table, the Earth
refines them between tooth-thinned trees.

Living Out of Jars

Now our dog is too loud—
enough is enough, the letter says.

Though anonymous,
I think, going by the handwriting,
I've narrowed it down
to the elderly couple
three houses away.

They save a share of each season
for the judging . . .
this is their philosophy, I suspect.

Shame for us is an oily car,
a broken mailbox,
an abundance of weeds—
a failure each day of the harvest.

They can slap their dried fruit gift basket
out of my hands themselves.

They Don't Want to Get This

      This high-rise apartment building   hasn't had a manager
in the lobby since 1979.   The last handler
left his plastic snake plants   bleaching olive
beside semi-gloss commissary paint
      back when the building   was at its most alive.

      Shows from RCAs and Philcos   captured pictures
of day to day life   and displayed them, legs and skin,
onto the building's drywall   (the actors weren't always naked
but became so even when clothed)   and residents on any floor
sensed the actors' lack of pants   by the method of their walking
past the doors on floor nine.

      Floor nine had leftover soap   from jellyfish-colored bubbles blown
off the AstroTurfed balcony   at the top of Annandale where purple
matchbox Pontiacs   shot through a paper towel tube,
rushed tenants far away from the building   at least to balloon's length,
clean through to junipers and sages   hues not used once anywhere
in the entire building's space.

      Level seven had a trash compactor   that was friends,
perhaps, with the elevators   and seemed to glow a temper
like roasted tomatoes   with its inner walls caramelizing garbage
on the way to the basement   and sometimes made more pleasant
by stripes of hard peppermint suckers.

      Hundreds of Sunday dinners   of Korean and Italian garlics
commixing with warm detergent   from level one's laundromat
couldn't block the dumpster's dirty banana-diaper reek
from baking fire-red film   into the elevator doors,
except for a couple of years   janitors wiped back the beige.

And the three elevators   were like the thick hand
that blindly pawed for candy   from a bowl
but the bowl was actually a brown clutch
from the pawn shop   and the quarters and jeons
were the bribes   and the hands
those hands   were the hands.

Components for Living a Perfect Life, Part III

Because we rise on the 4th of July
in plastic tambourine attire jingling
past needles of ornamental blue spruce
and quilts of crocheted, man-made lakes and cream

cheese desserts in flag shapes, past our ketchup
blotches masked by our burgundy blouses,
we should find our escape whenever
we can, under our highway bypasses,

by buckles of car-shopping indecision,
during public, perfunctory fire shows—
talented prodigies lost in the paint
of mustard life. Shaking crosettes

will sweat in the firepits of jealous neighbors
who later soak in pools for days and long joys.
We will reapply our tea tree repellant—
put our sweetened youth to bed.

Rhubarbs Between Roses

Herald De Ruiter's sturgeon beauty—
cherry suede dueled

against lovable florals—
collegiate Graham Thomas.

Grown together to make pleasant
chit-chat—first like murmured skin

then like vinegar—plucking at the other's reveries:
classic cornflower vs. wistful orchid.

Usher plush mediators—
Buff Beauties and Lavender Lassies—

a frank referee—Felicity. On the fissures
between roses the hybrids banding

for unity—Vanity, too, in all seasons
thorny turfs breed roughhousing.

Prayer

We beg to be   acceptable
as insects, first.
We promise to grow
more human-like,
to your liking.
We ask you
to ponder the bugs
    who change
    their shapes
from Hellgrammite
to Dobson Fly   adjust
from pincer
    to mandible.
We've changed   like they did,
    from Philipé
to Philip,
Mac Douglas
    to Douglas,
like tiny Puritans
secreting husk-shaped
    mounds,
    like Pilgrimmite
to Pilgrim
or Colonnite
    to Colonist.
  Bless our vetted cornucopias.
We pray their sound
is sonorous
enough to be   acceptable
  to your liking.
We'll offer fluttering
    hymnals sung
in supplication.
Like your beauty star
    butterflies,
we have done it for years.

Dying Country

One should not wash their hands by the river
        of a disintegrating country—where the water's
        rush may pull for dirt
        from under the fingernails, and together
        with the spirits, advance
        corrosion of the nation.

Do not desire to plant the bulbs of daffodils,
        not in this country's
        neglected states and fields.

Do not fill barrels with the seeds
        which will shrivel
        even before the end of April.

To believe in a dying country's memorabilia
        is to picture events, possessions,
        and knick-knacks washing up
        upon the shore:
        keychains, cedar boxes,
        church picnics, and Fat Tuesdays.

Don't look into the reflection
        of its evaporating water.
Do not attempt to scavenge from its land
        what is left of you,
        especially as its killers
        smash themselves into the sand.

Productive

Go through the letters,
throw at least half of them away.
Wait, then deal with the letters left.
This may take some time.

Bring something delicious to eat, too,
maybe not so salty, not meat.
We've been eating too much meat.

And the door, the door is broken again,
so tighten the screws.
Though the frame is breaking,
get a new door.
Call someone.

It's not my fault.
We've become utilitarian.

Thinking on that, not offended yet,
not yet, but,
use things   use of things
use of us. Do I use you?
You *want* me to use you?

Right now, there's something downstairs,
something to do, but not yet.
I forgot. It's not our fault
the bed is the sleeping place.

Progression

The children have the entire pool to themselves
        while I have the sidewalk deck around it   and the music

     which remind me of how we do nothing together

and it's playing   like a water horizon   easing toward the white and blue
       ceramic lines of tile   like depth perception in sound

and the shifty melody
and the lifeguards controlling the outdoor speakers

       the sounds which I swish with my toe-tap count   like I count the tile's grout divisions
       which match the pattern of the sun's on-water shimmer

which match the slow   concave/convex whipping

     of the stripes on the umbrella

and me, I'm like a drowning woman,

       and I'm becoming warm, still,   despite the shadow of the nylon shell
                  and the summer wind   turning us down

like the aqua tone of turquoise if it were chipped

             from the tile patterns

or from a fluid canvas wavering in measures.

Before She Got Away

The extraction will not
  come from a weaponized knife,
but from a lifelong surgery,
  where the tongue first gives up
playing a part in the philosophy
  of being a tongue, then a doctor holds it
between two fingers like sharks pacified
  by being twisted onto their backs

which marine biologists remind us
  is not dreadful for sharks—or so
they believe—but in this case,
  women being not of the ocean
or even a species perfected
  for millions of years that holds just this

flaw of being stunned into docility
  so easily, is actually, most painful
to the taste when so paralyzed. And this
  process of losing is when the first
protective coating of the tongue melts (just
  a little) in kiss-off of the dorsum's

plea to find a new mouth. The seasoning
  of this coating remains unknown. All flavors
from here on out are too bland
  or hot, or without sense of medium.
Some degree of all women's removal
  should be each woman's

which may whistle a bit within the watered
        hum of their exposed cords.
And there is a trap sewn for her
        into a man's back pocket where the tongue
lasts longer than the women—
        a temporary comfort.

Good Girl

I have shown you
all my brain contains.

First, the English plucked from Persia
a mastery of the walnut—
and made it their own.
In this way,
it's like the English calculated,
in rudimentary, imitation math,
how to claim
both sides of the brain,
and through this, the walnut's symmetry.

Maybe grasping the mini, unwashed fuzz
behind the hound's head is better
than the walnut's histories and grooves—
short-haired, she avoids these patterns.

Maybe her bony crown creates a pinnacle,
which allows her thinkings
to retract into the backdrop
of her canine mind.
And, this alone
balances right and left lobes.

It's good,
how she will not worry
for English or for ancient Persia
the way I do.
There's always a moment of tranquility
about this particular animal head—
the fur that covers her skull.

This is the last thing
I needed to tell you.

Components for Living a Perfect Life, Part IV

Because we don't know what we have
we must catch amen in old records—
our history of voices, press one to continue
and zero for only hums of each other.

Because we link like saffron
between strangers.
Because the other way
is living to keep others from dying.

Because we want to play in opal
fields overrun by bee balm,
and dwell free
as clean suburban clerics.

We should persist in electricity,
once and for all, not
run from falling down sycamores
in front of the playing children.

Recognized as Insect Elsewhere

"He felt as if he were being shown the way to the unknown nourishment he longed for."

--Franz Kafka, *The Metamorphosis*

I went to the bookstore,
       and nothing happened.
I thought I'd meet Purpose in the aisle,
       my long lost . . .

       O, this spiritual union with creator of stardust!
       Singularity! Quasar! Muse!
       Your illumination blinding readers in aisles four and five—
       Your voice, angelic, bellowing past crackle of damp intercom—
       Fluorescent bulbs exploding with the magnitude . . .

A woman my age has a child who does not like my child.
I scuttle from the bookstore wearing more than two legs.
I crawl into my car.

My tarsal claws
       hold down the pages,
my compound eyes
       probe for our names.

American Concubine

Berlin collected the greatest porcelain
and ruled with the spiral meat of Easter.
I am leftovers and Haviland patterns
scorched into coccyx.

Undressed, I build countertops,
mix pastings from piles. My sacrum
of disturbed ground
neither trustworthy, nor trusting.

No more trust. My vertebrae renovate
by sexing upon shards of Europe's antique goods.
Self-proclaimed thief and concubine,
I build marble suburbs out of common bones.

For Modernism: First Impressions of War

When I met you at the museum,
I understood you best. I loved you
when I was four feet high:
a Minimalist, an early Symbolist.

I adored you for expressing
my awkwardness,
my bleak and stark—a Brutalist.
I was mostly animal, like you,
abstracted—as splattered and crumbled
as you—cubed onto walls of concrete.

Dot to gallery room,
line to gallery room,
paintings of one solid, purple square,
light from three stories of windows—
the 20th century collectors say you
understand me, and I you.

Because we scuffled from trench
to marble floor
and from pasture
into shrapnel petals.
Because we did not know what to do
but splinter into scumbled new.

Only within the radius of your exhibits,
from the bleach of struck atriums,
could you spill a still life's
spores into an over-boil of paint.
We are from one Klee brush;
we are one girl grasping Picasso, best.
And the wars that spawned us,
they canvass on forever.

Spores on Postcards

I took you out
on a summer Wednesday
for ice cream at the mini-mart,
but on the way there
we drove by a black bird and a mushroom
lined up on the pine-needled rise,
stilted like a photochrome postcard.

Then, I may have imagined that the raven
danced around that mushroom,
just as I dreamed up a life for the man
who crossed the sidewalk in front of us
to buy Mountain Dew and Basics.

His friend waited in a rusty Impala—
both men kept some secret
that warped their smiles.
By the time he walked by our picnic table,
I'd eaten the last of the sprinkles.

Simultaneously, I imagined
the raven and the Lepiota—
the men like the raven
and me like the eyeless air
that watches mushrooms rise.

How the raven seemed to plot
over the organic fabric
at the base of the mushroom.
How he was an oily bird
casing the size and space,
posing, reposing
on his orange little sticks,
caw-singing a forest voodoo.

I let the men steal some of the beauty
of that bird, as all of us stood
uneven in the rule of thirds,
our beaks and lips.

To Avoid Vacuuming

I think about my mother's European nose:
about her enjoying the streets of Paris
when she was younger than I am now.
I think of floating by the Eiffel Tower
in a hot air balloon
called *The Cheery Death Trap,*
its crisp twinkles of nylon
bubbling into the horizon,
and just before the accident,
when its skin ruptures magnificent rainbow
across the warp of land,
I slip into that ammolite city.

Components for Living a Perfect Life, Part V

We could gather together to dust off knick-knack
mantels stacked with spoons and yarn dolls,
knit scarves and caps with seasoned hands.
Because no one has to suffer watching the news

or paw in the dark for keychains. We don't
break; we do not misinform our young ones.
We could expunge ourselves by a river
of ph-balanced water, untangle

our copper coils—the repurposed barrels
bobbing in plastic spoilage. We would return
heart lockets of young Elvis, walk out
from the childhood of burn-wilted, prudish

America. Then we'd remember where
we put the little girls we were when we
were through with being one of them. Where we
could walk away, even from those we love.

Welling Up

You never want these disruptions—
you mean to weep alone above

the hollow mouth, the quiet between
whistles of birds your irritant,

your shame like the moss
the metal bucket rips from the stone wall

dragging leaves into its mob of debris,
and booming bog at its shale base.

And when you return, you'll be fine
until someone asks. Then that compassion,

pungent and suffocating, breaking
into admission of sentiment, will water

like an allergy of blue dune wheat into silver.
You cannot expect to get away from this water.

Elongation

Thinking of northern places
makes her dizzy lids

want to burrow through the gelid
to the end of skies.

She eyes a precipice,
just a distant cartography.

She pilots her walking,
calculates latitude cracks,

city footpaths—loses count—
a sidewalk must have an end.

She believes northbound concrete
can only lead to Canada, or cold-fish

shades of blue sky, or to splintered piers
stacking surface onto water. She wonders

how land hides its height
in the fog at Saint John's Bay—

why the heedless geese mock her
with winged elation. Why they pocket

into the pulling whip of undertow tide—
still, she moves north—

her cold feet touching the longitude tightrope,
the thinning air rising

like its own balloon—propelling her above glacier—

up and up again, in increments, with the precision of eagles.

She swears, now, this is the end of Earth
and Nova Scotia, where the edges

roll into cotta dough of pine terrain—
the land strands stretching into transparency,

to where wandering boreal
eats snow-covered Taiga.

Elegy for the Bird Killed in the Parking Lot at St. Edward the Confessor's

Church does not save
a misplaced robin (bundled) in the parking spot,
cold in his feathers, tired, parent bird,
oblivious to tires—to the involuntary van
in front of us. We had just learned
about forgiveness.

At that moment: it was miserable
for the robin, too—all was undone.
I could not mourn the bird
correctly, not in front of you, knowing
you are a child learning about the universe.
And it was an accident. Even God
did not mean to let us
see him burst.

During the Variety Show

    This is the shuffle of bodies

            cramped between the bluing tubes

    fidgeting under the weight,

        under the stone muzzles, the oily orbs.

Come here.

    This is the suffer of star-charts,

young static shock beneath TV light,

    perverted silhouettes

        warped ad slogans in Klinkomite font.

Someone should fear these scuttles

        under bobble squares,

    fear a 50s re-run bow-tied host

broadcasting big band civility

    ignoring transmissions of the outer banshee.

Now why so uneasy?

Passing by the Lichgate

     In the Baptist graveyard,
a woman with a bright, long blonde wig
tends to plastic flowers.

The acre has no fence, just two
freestanding brick
columns connected by

the Lichgate's iron, the stock
gate of earth-heavy
protection of black and brick

of blue and sky
God allusions
of the Godless, adorned

by eternal lilies, silken
heavenly perfection
her ache and hover over

the dead, roaming just past
the lichgate, dangling
her locks above bevel markers

in her electric blue blouse,
the honey perfume and sweat drip
without reason to bathe for the dead.

Tracking the Storm

When the bands come
she creates a safe cage,
encloses the toddler body,
sets aside her wet chest and ribs.

With or without steady memories
of the boy, clearing delivers
blue from other coasts.

She's sorry, then,
to speak of her own weather.
The flooding comes often, too,
to other towns.

It's before the hurricane
that they split into sprigs.

From the Third-floor Apartment
Cambridge, Massachusetts

I wrestled to ease heaven
screeching through the drywall and concrete
while the new weather wired up the bends of the fire escape.
The breeze approaching the cord
ethered in some colonial zephyr . . .

    That howl tethered me
    to the wharfing island
    and fixed me to old winters.

    I heard wayfarers:
    a Mayflower docking in the Mystic,
    a tired bow tapping on the cobblestone,
    the mass rocking its hook
    and straddling frost.

    I pictured the balconies now as planks
    and the air without obstacle to slow it.
    The whole of the Cape contused in unison—
    urban waxed to ship,
    splinter creaked to crescendo.

    If I had not been too cowardly
    to look out the window,
    I thought I might see pilgrims
    manifesting their boarding at the shore—
    their patience struck-through in the forecastle.
    I, too, shivered, hoping the buoyancy would pass.

It seemed we continued to lug. I returned
to daydreams of modern drinkers,
toasting, perhaps, and unaware at River Gods—
how the bar's water hosts might flounder
without land to girder them.

Until the lapse departed,
I kept my eyes closed,
knowing that if I looked down,
I might see the ocean swell
surging across the sidewalk.

Pretending to Be a Stingray

Enjoying your morning glory mind
as ocean,
as motile as the diving gull,
you mosey
        the treeless green-blue—
              feel rain seeds touch the ceiling
        of sea, then watch them ricochet to shadow.

Your mother loves to know
that your tiny feet fit
into the world of gliding
as able as any of those beveled birds
and roaming fish.

When your legs are grown
you run free and upright in the street
but your mother can't confirm
the words
              which best describe
       how you came
             to play this way.

Lava Song

I've got you, Lava.
I coveted you once like I would
        the vertical rushfoil.

I found you where you once lived—
        poppy-neon and unfinished
        like a lanceolate in hell.

I've found you, Lava—
        when the rostrum lights play you
        in punches of color.
You are fever, not vera.

I still hold you, Lava,
        while meek Vesuvians
        ask for water.
I know you in linear, in spear,
        and in stained glass.

Legitimate heat associates
        this much hex with evil.

        It's not your fault,
you're divided by the blackened lead came
        that kilns your magenta and geranium.
And I'm just now reaching
        the fuchsia edges.

Notes

Epigraph from "Freedom of Speech" from *Stay, Illusion.* Copyright © 2013 by Lucie Brock-Broido. Published by Alfred A. Knopf, Inc. an imprint of The Knopf Doubleday Publishing Group, a division of Random House LLC.

"Fishing-kids' Rock Seat": References a pyramid pile of concrete left behind by the townhouse construction builders when they made Huntsman Lake located in Northern Virginia. Conveniently placed at a thumb of land caught between the creek and the lake itself, the rock pile became a proverbial king of the hill or prime seat for fishing. Roughly two to three people could manage seating it at any given time.

"Recognized as Insect Elsewhere": Refers to Franz Kafka's *The Metamorphosis.* Also called "Die Verwandlung," "The Transformation," published in German as *Die Verwandlung* in 1915.

"Tracking the Storm": Motivated by Hurricane Isabel, which hit Richmond, Virginia in 2003.

ACKNOWLEDGMENTS

Many thanks to the magazines and journals that gave these poems their first home, some appearing in a different form:

The Pinch Issue 38.1 "Experiment of a Woman as a Paper Cut-out"
Parentheses Issue 02 "Mustard Originelle"
Whurk Magazine "Sarcastic Prayer"
Passengers Journal "American Concubine"
Lily Poetry Review "Elongation"
Lingering in the Margins "Elegy for the Bird Killed in the Parking Lot at St. Edward the Confessor's"

I am deeply grateful for the generosity and support of mentors, teachers, and poets, especially Adrian Matejka, Kevin Prufer, Erin Belieu, Joan Houlihan, and Carolyn Kreiter-Foronda. A special thanks to the Lesley University MFA program, where I met my wonderful writing family: Michelle Boland, Aaron Wallace, Michael Lynch, Caitlin Robinson, Rex Arrasmith, Robbie Gamble, Michelle Ramadan, Frances Donovan, Julie Cyr, Michael Mercurio, Natalie Young, Aqueela Britt, and so many other amazing writers, but especially to Dan Kakitis.

Thank you to the writing community of Richmond, Virginia: Dale Brumfield, Joanna Lee, Guy Terrell; to the English department of Meadowbrook High School, to Kristin Thrower, and to the River City Poets.

Thank you, Eileen Cleary and Christine Jones for believing in my work and for the commitment of expertise and time they lent to this project.

Thank you for lifelong friendships: especially Brandy Barents and Kevin Barents. Also, Wendy Lively, Debbie Amos, Kerra English, When-Dee Morrison, Bonnie Natale, Beth Hart, Kelly Kerr, and Shannon & Drew Wickham for unconditional support.

Finally, thank you to my parents, Verena and Jasper Lupo. I'm grateful for the love of Vince & Kyla Lupo, Lawrence Lupo, and finally, for the many hours of sacrifice and patience: Mark Adkins, Linda Adkins, Katherine, Daniel, and Eric.

ABOUT THE AUTHOR

Clarissa Adkins lives in Richmond, Virginia and earned degrees from James Madison University and Lesley University. As a high school English teacher, she co-coordinates her school's Poetry Out Loud program and is a teacher action researcher, exploring culturally responsive teaching practices with Virginia Commonwealth University's Metropolitan Educational Research Consortium. Clarissa's published in *The Pinch, Whurk Magazine,* River City Poets' anthology: *Lingering in the Margins, Passengers Journal,* and more. She earned a Best of the Net nomination from Parentheses International Literary Arts Journal and was a finalist for the 17th Annual Erskine J. Poetry Prize. She reads for *Sugar House Review.*

www.ingramcontent.com/pod-product-compliance
Lightning Source LLC
LaVergne TN
LVHW041650060526
838200LV00040B/1787